Pra

and what Would Faith Do?

"'Life does not happen to you!' is just one of the quotes by Faith Young, creator of this amazing journal, designed to inspire and empower you. The *What Would Faith Do? Journal* is all about making things happen and being grateful every day for what you currently have so you can create the future you want. This journal is like no other because it is laid out to make it easy for you to state your intentions and your daily gratitude. Once you use this, you will see more positivity in your life and be on your way to creating the life you always wanted. Life does not happen to you… you make it happen!"

- Lesli Hassell

"I love, LOVE the *What Would Faith Do? Journal*! It help me to show love for myself and things I love about me when in the past, it was difficult to see. It also helped me set my intention for each day and celebrate my daily accomplishments. So exciting!"

- Sophie Marie,
What Would Faith Do? Workshop participant

"Faith Young is not just an inspiring author, she is an inspiring person. You will find nuggets of inspiration and ways to change the way you look at life. Faith isn't just a person, she is a living demonstration of her namesake. One of the things I enjoy about this journal is that each meme seems to be the exact message I need for the day. Namaste."

Mythica Von Griffyn,
Author of *Power of Pretend* & SkinWars TV Star

"Have you often wondered what it would take to change your life? Then you have come to the right place. Faith Young is the guru of walking you through how easy it is to change your life by changing the way you think. Everyday live a life of gratitude. That is where it all begins.

Faith Young divinely showed up in my life and nothing was ever the same after that. I am not the person I was at our first meeting. I have changed my world by following her instructions and advice.

In less than a year, I became a published author, a motivational speaker and so much more. I have learned to love myself at every step of my journey. I am alive again. I am laughing and loving more often and so much deeper. There is now color in my world.

The *What Would Faith Do? Journal* will keep you on track daily by having you live consciously. You will soon notice all you have to be grateful for. It enhances your love for yourself by being aware about who you are and what makes you special. It guides you to have intention for your day so you will stay on track while on your way to your destiny and so much more.

Get ready for an amazing ride!"

- Jill Bill, Popular Author of "Nine Hours to Goodbye"

This Journal Belongs To: _____

What Would Faith Do? Journal

Young, Faith, Author
What Would Faith Do? Journal
Faith Young

ISBN: 978-1-5394-3056-8

JOURNAL

QUANTITY PURCHASES: Schools, companies, professional
groups, clubs, and other organizations may qualify for
special terms when ordering quantities of this title.
For information, email Faith@WhatWouldFaithDo.com

With a heart full of gratitude, I dedicate this journal
to each and every person who has believed in me
throughout my life's journey. Through the power of
faith all things are made possible. Thank you for
believing in me. I love and appreciate
you more than you will ever know.

Note to the Reader

Hello my friend! My intention with this journal is to make a positive impact in this world by sharing my story and the action steps I have been implementing in my own life on a daily basis.

"We can have 100 things go right, and we tend to focus on the ONE that went wrong!"

I discovered that we as humans tend to focus on what we don't want. And what we think about, we bring about. With the beautiful power of the Law of Attraction, it is more important than ever to focus on what we do want.

My "What Would Faith Do? Journal" is designed for this very reason. To allow you to stop focusing on what you don't want and start getting clear on what you do want in your life. My Power of Faith worksheet is a proven way to celebrate all the gifts in your life on a daily basis.

In my "What Would Faith Do?" Book I share the story of how I changed my negative thoughts into positive thoughts, eliminated blame and took ownership, and most importantly changed my attitude about my life to create this magical life I've always wanted.

This journal will help you do this very thing. So, are you ready to attract more love & abundance into your life? Do you want more happiness? Are you tired of things being hard or taking so long to show up? Well, take action today. I challenge you to fill out this journal each and every day to stop the vicious cycle and start positively impacting your life and the other lives around you today.

Your story matters. Once the gifts start showing up, share your story on my What Would Faith Do? The Journal fan page on Facebook. Better yet, want to inspire others? Take a photo of your journal page and post in on social media daily with your favorite hashtag #WWFD!

Let the magic begin....

With love & abundance,

Faith Young

Faith :
creating space for
something that you
might not see
as possible.
- Faith Young

www.OunceofFaith.com

Date: _____

_____
_____
_____
_____
_____
_____
_____
_____
_____
_____
_____
_____
_____
_____
_____

5 things I am grateful for:

5 things I love about me:

My intention:

My Successes:

What have I manifested or what will I
attract into my life today:

What Powerful connection will or did I make
today?

The Power of Faith

The grass is greener
wherever you water it!

Faith Young

www.OunceOfFaith.com

Date: _____

_____

_____

_____

_____

_____

_____

_____

_____

_____

_____

_____

_____

_____

_____

_____

Faith Young - The Journal

5 things I am grateful for:

5 things I love about me:

My intention:

My successes:

What have I manifested or what will I
attract into my life today:

What powerful connection will or did I make
today?

The Power of Faith

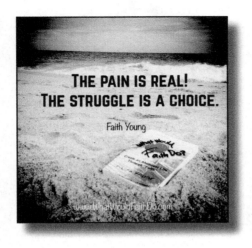

Date: _____

_____

_____

_____

_____

_____

_____

_____

_____

_____

_____

_____

_____

_____

_____

_____

_____

5 things I am grateful for:

5 things I love about me:

My intention:

My Successes:

What have I manifested or what will I
attract into my life today:

What powerful connection will or did I make
today?

The Power of Faith

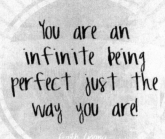

You are an
infinite being
perfect just the
way you are!

Faith Young

Date: _____

_____

_____

_____

_____

_____

_____

_____

_____

_____

_____

_____

_____

_____

_____

_____

What would Faith Do?

5 things I am grateful for:

5 things I love about me:

My intention:

My Successes:

What have I manifested or what will I attract into my life today:

What Powerful connection will or did I make today?

The Power of Faith

Be the Gift you are Seeking!

Faith Young

Date: _____

_____

_____

_____

_____

_____

_____

_____

_____

_____

_____

_____

_____

_____

_____

_____

5 things I am grateful for:

5 things I love about me:

My intention:

My Successes:

What have I manifested or what will I
attract into my life today:

What powerful connection will or did I make
today?

The Power of Faith

Be the Gift you are Seeking!

Faith Young

Date: _____

_____

_____

_____

_____

_____

_____

_____

_____

_____

_____

_____

_____

_____

_____

_____

Faith Young - The Journal

5 things I am grateful for:

5 things I love about me:

My intention:

My Successes:

What have I manifested or what will I
attract into my life today:

What powerful connection will or did I make
today?

The Power of Faith

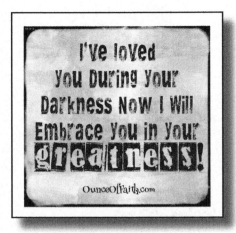

Date: _____

_____

_____

_____

_____

_____

_____

_____

_____

_____

_____

_____

_____

_____

_____

What would Faith Do?

5 things I am grateful for:

5 things I love about me:

My intention:

My Successes:

What have I manifested or what will I
attract into my life today:

What Powerful connection will or did I make
today?

The Power of Faith

Receive as if your Heart is counting On it!

FAITH YOUNG

Date: _____

_____

_____

_____

_____

_____

_____

_____

_____

_____

_____

_____

_____

_____

_____

_____

5 things I am grateful for:

5 things I love about me:

My intention:

My Successes:

What have I manifested or what will I attract into my life today:

What powerful connection will or did I make today?

The Power of Faith

We can have
100 things go right
And we tend to
focus on the
one
That went
wrong

fAith YOUNg

Date: _____

_____

_____

_____

_____

_____

_____

_____

_____

_____

_____

_____

_____

_____

_____

_____

5 things I am grateful for:

5 things I love about me:

My intention:

My successes:

What have I manifested or what will I
attract into my life today:

What powerful connection will or did I make
today?

The Power of Faith

Your wings already exist
all you have to do is take the leap of Faith!

- Faith Young

WWFD.me

Date: _____

_____
_____
_____
_____
_____
_____
_____
_____
_____
_____
_____
_____
_____
_____
_____
_____

Faith Young - The Journal

5 things I am grateful for:

5 things I love about me:

My intention:

My successes:

What have I manifested or what will I
attract into my life today:

What powerful connection will or did I make
today?

The Power of Faith

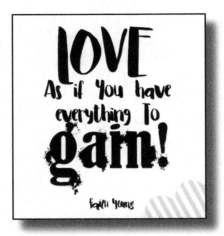

Date: _____

_____
_____
_____
_____
_____
_____
_____
_____
_____
_____
_____
_____
_____
_____
_____
_____

5 things I am grateful for:

5 things I love about me:

My intention:

My successes:

What have I manifested or what will I
attract into my life today:

What powerful connection will or did I make
today?

The Power of Faith

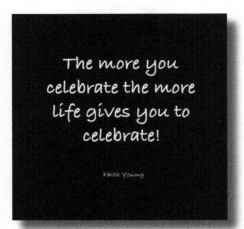

The more you celebrate the more life gives you to celebrate!

Faith Young

Date: _____

_____
_____
_____
_____
_____
_____
_____
_____
_____
_____
_____
_____
_____
_____
_____

what would Faith Do?

5 things I am grateful for:

5 things I love about me:

My intention:

My successes:

What have I manifested or what will I
attract into my life today:

What powerful connection will or did I make
today?

The Power of Faith

Date: _____

_____

_____

_____

_____

_____

_____

_____

_____

_____

_____

_____

_____

_____

_____

_____

_____

what would Faith Do?

5 things I am grateful for:

5 things I love about me:

My intention:

My Successes:

What have I manifested or what will I
attract into my life today:

What Powerful connection will or did I make
today?

The Power of Faith

"I never underestimate the power of the little things I do each and every day and how they can powerfully impact someone's life!"

FAITH YOUNG

Date: _____

_____

_____

_____

_____

_____

_____

_____

_____

_____

_____

_____

_____

_____

_____

_____

Faith Young - The Journal

what would Faith Do?

5 things I am grateful for:

5 things I love about me:

MY intention:

MY successes:

What have I manifested or what will I
attract into my life today:

What powerful connection will or did I make
today?

The Power of Faith

> Being able to bring
> the light out of the
> darkness is pure magic.
>
> Faith Young

Date: _____

_____

_____

_____

_____

_____

_____

_____

_____

_____

_____

_____

_____

_____

Faith Young - The Journal

5 things I am grateful for:

5 things I love about me:

My intention:

My successes:

What have I manifested or what will I
attract into my life today:

What powerful connection will or did I make
today?

The Power of Faith

the
ONLY ReASON
you got
haters
is cuz
you got
game

Faith Young

Date: _____

_____
_____
_____
_____
_____
_____
_____
_____
_____
_____
_____
_____
_____
_____
_____

Faith Young - The Journal

What would Faith Do?

5 things I am grateful for:

5 things I love about me:

My intention:

My successes:

What have I manifested or what will I attract into my life today:

What powerful connection will or did I make today?

The Power of Faith

When you
are Traveling
remind yourself
you always Arrive
happy & well

faith young

Date: _____

_____
_____
_____
_____
_____
_____
_____
_____
_____
_____
_____
_____
_____
_____
_____
_____

5 things I am grateful for:

5 things I love about me:

My intention:

My Successes:

What have I manifested or what will I
attract into my life today:

What Powerful connection will or did I make
today?

The Power of Faith

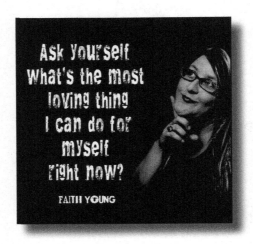

Ask Yourself
What's the most
loving thing
I can do for
myself
right now?

FAITH YOUNG

Date: _____

_____
_____
_____
_____
_____
_____
_____
_____
_____
_____
_____
_____
_____
_____

Faith Young - The Journal

5 things I am grateful for:

5 things I love about me:

My intention:

My Successes:

What have I manifested or what will I
attract into my life today:

What powerful connection will or did I make
today?

The Power of Faith

You'll never regret
spending time doing
what makes you happy!

Faith Young

Date: _____

_____
_____
_____
_____
_____
_____
_____
_____
_____
_____
_____
_____
_____
_____
_____
_____

5 things I am grateful for:

5 things I love about me:

My intention:

My successes:

What have I manifested or what will I
attract into my life today:

What powerful connection will or did I make
today?

The Power of Faith

Love has no boundaries or limitations. When it's meant to be it will find you!

Faith Young

Date: _____

_____

_____

_____

_____

_____

_____

_____

_____

_____

_____

_____

_____

_____

_____

_____

Faith Young - The Journal

5 things I am grateful for:

5 things I love about me:

My intention:

My successes:

What have I manifested or what will I
attract into my life today:

What powerful connection will or did I make
today?

The Power of Faith

DO WHATEVER
MAKES YOU
HAPPY!

Faith Young

Date: _____

_____
_____
_____
_____
_____
_____
_____
_____
_____
_____
_____
_____
_____
_____
_____

5 things I am grateful for:

5 things I love about me:

My intention:

My Successes:

What have I manifested or what will I
attract into my life today:

What powerful connection will or did I make
today?

The Power of Faith

When you look
up to your hero realize
someone else is looking up
to you in this same way.

Faith Young

Date: _____

_____

_____

_____

_____

_____

_____

_____

_____

_____

_____

_____

_____

_____

_____

5 things I am grateful for:

5 things I love about me:

My intention:

My Successes:

What have I manifested or what will I
attract into my life today:

What Powerful connection will or did I make
today?

The Power of Faith

I have more Faith in you
than you can imagine!
When in doubt
ask yourself
What Would Faith Do?

Faith Young

Date: _____

_____

_____

_____

_____

_____

_____

_____

_____

_____

_____

_____

_____

_____

_____

5 things I am grateful for:

5 things I love about me:

My intention:

My successes:

What have I manifested or what will I
attract into my life today:

What powerful connection will or did I make
today?

The Power of Faith

You have to believe in magic if you want magic to start showing up!

Faith Young

Date: _____

_____

_____

_____

_____

_____

_____

_____

_____

_____

_____

_____

_____

_____

_____

5 things I am grateful for:

5 things I love about me:

My intention:

My successes:

What have I manifested or what will I
attract into my life today:

What powerful connection will or did I make
today?

The Power of Faith

You have
to believe
in magic if
you want
magic to start
showing up!

Faith Young

Date: _____

_____

_____

_____

_____

_____

_____

_____

_____

_____

_____

_____

_____

_____

_____

_____

5 things I am grateful for:

5 things I love about me:

My intention:

My successes:

What have I manifested or what will I
attract into my life today:

What powerful connection will or did I make
today?

The Power of Faith

worrying just brings you more shit to worry about

Faith Young

Date: _____

_____

_____

_____

_____

_____

_____

_____

_____

_____

_____

_____

_____

_____

_____

_____

5 things I am grateful for:

5 things I love about me:

My intention:

My successes:

What have I manifested or what will I attract into my life today:

What powerful connection will or did I make today?

The Power of Faith

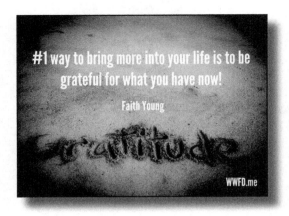

#1 way to bring more into your life is to be grateful for what you have now!

Faith Young

gratitude

WWFD.me

Date: _____

_____

_____

_____

_____

_____

_____

_____

_____

_____

_____

_____

_____

_____

_____

Faith Young - The Journal

5 things I am grateful for:

5 things I love about me:

My intention:

My successes:

What have I manifested or what will I
attract into my life today:

What powerful connection will or did I make
today?

The Power of Faith

Date: _____

_____
_____
_____
_____
_____
_____
_____
_____
_____
_____
_____
_____
_____
_____
_____
_____

what would Faith Do?

5 things I am grateful for:

5 things I love about me:

my intention:

my successes:

What have I manifested or what will I attract into my life today:

What powerful connection will or did I make today?

The Power of Faith

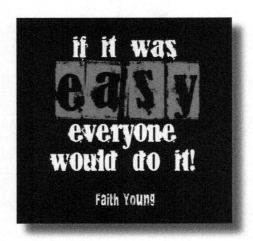

Date: _____

_____

_____

_____

_____

_____

_____

_____

_____

_____

_____

_____

_____

_____

_____

5 things I am grateful for:

5 things I love about me:

My intention:

My Successes:

What have I manifested or what will I attract into my life today:

What powerful connection will or did I make today?

The Power of Faith

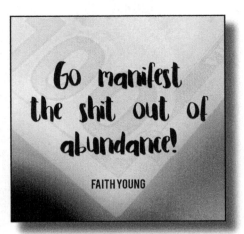

Go manifest
the shit out of
abundance!

FAITH YOUNG

Date: _____

_____

_____

_____

_____

_____

_____

_____

_____

_____

_____

_____

_____

_____

_____

_____

_____

5 things I am grateful for:

5 things I love about me:

my intention:

my successes:

What have I manifested or what will I
attract into my life today:

What powerful connection will or did I make
today?

The Power of Faith

What's holding
you back from
doing what you really
want to do in life?

www.OunceOffaith.com

Date: _____

_____

_____

_____

_____

_____

_____

_____

_____

_____

_____

_____

_____

_____

_____

_____

Faith Young - The Journal

5 things I am grateful for:

5 things I love about me:

My intention:

My successes:

What have I manifested or what will I
attract into my life today:

What powerful connection will or did I make
today?

The Power of Faith

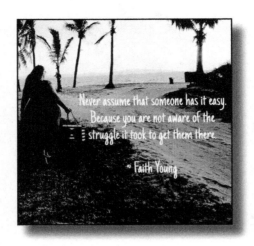

Never assume that someone has it easy. Because you are not aware of the struggle it took to get them there.

— Faith Young

Date: _____

_____

_____

_____

_____

_____

_____

_____

_____

_____

_____

_____

_____

_____

_____

_____

What Would Faith Do?

5 things I am grateful for:

5 things I love about me:

My intention:

My Successes:

What have I manifested or what will I attract into my life today:

What Powerful connection will or did I make today?

The Power of Faith

All things are
possible through
The Power of
FAITH
www.OunceOfFaith.com

Date: _____

_____

_____

_____

_____

_____

_____

_____

_____

_____

_____

_____

_____

_____

_____

_____

_____

5 things I am grateful for:

5 things I love about me:

My intention:

My successes:

What have I manifested or what will I
attract into my life today:

What powerful connection will or did I make
today?

The Power of Faith

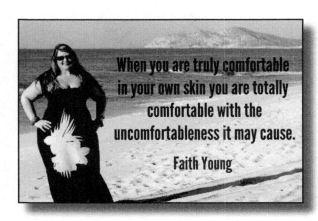

When you are truly comfortable in your own skin you are totally comfortable with the uncomfortableness it may cause.

Faith Young

Date: _____

_____

_____

_____

_____

_____

_____

_____

_____

_____

_____

_____

_____

_____

_____

_____

5 things I am grateful for:

5 things I love about me:

My intention:

My successes:

What have I manifested or what will I attract into my life today:

What powerful connection will or did I make today?

The Power of Faith

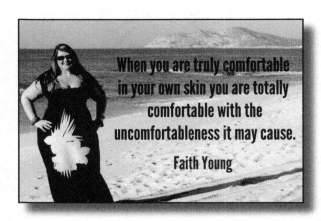

When you are truly comfortable in your own skin you are totally comfortable with the uncomfortableness it may cause.

Faith Young

Date: _____

_____

_____

_____

_____

_____

_____

_____

_____

_____

_____

_____

_____

_____

_____

_____

5 things I am grateful for:

5 things I love about me:

My intention:

My Successes:

What have I manifested or what will I
attract into my life today:

What powerful connection will or did I make
today?

The Power of Faith

May your week be filled
Magic!

Faith Young

WWFD.me

Date: _____

_____

_____

_____

_____

_____

_____

_____

_____

_____

_____

_____

_____

_____

_____

_____

_____

5 things I am grateful for:

5 things I love about me:

My intention:

My Successes:

What have I manifested or what will I
attract into my life today:

What powerful connection will or did I make
today?

The Power of Faith

has anyone told you today that you are a badass?

ENJOY THE PROCESS

www.OunceOfFaith.com

Date: _____

_____
_____
_____
_____
_____
_____
_____
_____
_____
_____
_____
_____
_____
_____
_____
_____
_____
_____

what would Faith Do?

5 things I am grateful for:

5 things I love about me:

My intention:

My successes:

What have I manifested or what will I attract into my life today:

What powerful connection will or did I make today?

The Power of Faith

The more abundance I attract into my life the more people's lives I can touch.

Faith Young

www.WhatWouldFaithDo.com

Date: _____

_____

_____

_____

_____

_____

_____

_____

_____

_____

_____

_____

_____

_____

_____

_____

_____

5 things I am grateful for:

5 things I love about me:

My intention:

My successes:

What have I manifested or what will I attract into my life today:

What powerful connection will or did I make today?

The Power of Faith

Date: _____

_____

_____

_____

_____

_____

_____

_____

_____

_____

_____

_____

_____

_____

_____

_____

_____

What would Faith Do?

5 things I am grateful for:

5 things I love about me:

My intention:

My successes:

What have I manifested or what will I attract into my life today:

What powerful connection will or did I make today?

The Power of Faith

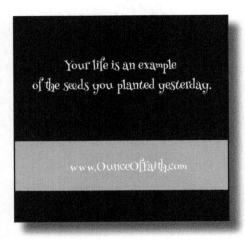

Your life is an example
of the seeds you planted yesterday.

www.OunceOfFaith.com

Date: _____

_____

_____

_____

_____

_____

_____

_____

_____

_____

_____

_____

_____

_____

_____

Faith Young - The Journal

5 things I am grateful for:

5 things I love about me:

My intention:

My successes:

What have I manifested or what will I
attract into my life today:

What powerful connection will or did I make
today?

The Power of Faith

'Faith it til you make it.'
Faith Young

Date: _____

_____
_____
_____
_____
_____
_____
_____
_____
_____
_____
_____
_____
_____
_____
_____

what would Faith Do?

5 things I am grateful for:

5 things I love about me:

MY intention:

MY successes:

What have I manifested or what will I
attract into my life today:

What powerful connection will or did I make
today?

The Power of Faith

SILENT GRATITUDE DOESN'T DO ANYONE ANY GOOD!
FAITH YOUNG

Date: _____

_____
_____
_____
_____
_____
_____
_____
_____
_____
_____
_____
_____
_____
_____
_____
_____

5 things I am grateful for:

5 things I love about me:

My intention:

My Successes:

What have I manifested or what will I
attract into my life today:

What Powerful connection will or did I make
today?

The Power of Faith

I receive
compliments graciously!

www.OunceOfFaith.com

Date: _____

_____

_____

_____

_____

_____

_____

_____

_____

_____

_____

_____

_____

_____

_____

_____

Faith Young - The Journal

5 things I am grateful for:

5 things I love about me:

my intention:

my successes:

What have I manifested or what will I
attract into my life today:

What powerful connection will or did I make
today?

The Power of Faith

Date: _____

_____

_____

_____

_____

_____

_____

_____

_____

_____

_____

_____

_____

_____

_____

_____

5 things I am grateful for:

5 things I love about me:

My intention:

My successes:

What have I manifested or what will I
attract into my life today:

What powerful connection will or did I make
today?

The Power of Faith

I'm pulling the weeds out
of my life so I have room for my
flowers to flourish!

www.OunceOfFaith.com

Date: _____

_____

_____

_____

_____

_____

_____

_____

_____

_____

_____

_____

_____

_____

What would Faith Do?

5 things I am grateful for:

5 things I love about me:

My intention:

My successes:

What have I manifested or what will I attract into my life today:

What powerful connection will or did I make today?

The Power of Faith

Date: _____

_____

_____

_____

_____

_____

_____

_____

_____

_____

_____

_____

_____

_____

_____

_____

5 things I am grateful for:

5 things I love about me:

My intention:

My Successes:

What have I manifested or what will I
attract into my life today:

What powerful connection will or did I make
today?

The Power of Faith

Date: _____

_____

_____

_____

_____

_____

_____

_____

_____

_____

_____

_____

_____

_____

_____

Faith Young - The Journal

5 things I am grateful for:

5 things I love about me:

My intention:

My successes:

What have I manifested or what will I
attract into my life today:

What Powerful connection will or did I make
today?

The Power of Faith

We ALL have the same 24 hours in a day. The only difference is what you choose to do with those hours.

FAITH YOUNG

Date: _____

_____
_____
_____
_____
_____
_____
_____
_____
_____
_____
_____
_____
_____
_____
_____
_____

5 things I am grateful for:

5 things I love about me:

My intention:

My successes:

What have I manifested or what will I attract into my life today:

What powerful connection will or did I make today?

The Power of Faith

To create space for
something you might not
see is possible.
This is the true essence of Faith!

FAITH YOUNG

WWFD.me

Date: _____

_____

_____

_____

_____

_____

_____

_____

_____

_____

_____

_____

_____

_____

_____

_____

_____

5 things I am grateful for:

5 things I love about me:

My intention:

My Successes:

What have I manifested or what will I attract into my life today:

What powerful connection will or did I make today?

The Power of Faith

Date: _____

_____
_____
_____
_____
_____
_____
_____
_____
_____
_____
_____
_____
_____
_____
_____

Faith Young - The Journal

5 things I am grateful for:

5 things I love about me:

My intention:

My successes:

What have I manifested or what will I
attract into my life today:

What powerful connection will or did I make
today?

The Power of Faith

Date: _____

_____

_____

_____

_____

_____

_____

_____

_____

_____

_____

_____

_____

_____

_____

_____

5 things I am grateful for:

5 things I love about me:

My intention:

My successes:

What have I manifested or what will I
attract into my life today:

What powerful connection will or did I make
today?

The Power of Faith

It's not about achieving your goals! It's about who you become on the journey to making them come true.

www.OunceOfFaith.com

Date: _____

_____

_____

_____

_____

_____

_____

_____

_____

_____

_____

_____

_____

_____

_____

5 things I am grateful for:

5 things I love about me:

My intention:

My Successes:

What have I manifested or what will I
attract into my life today:

What powerful connection will or did I make
today?

The Power of Faith

When you have something knock you off track
write 100 things you are grateful for:

_____

_____

_____

_____

_____

_____

_____

_____

_____

_____

_____

_____

_____

_____

_____

_____

_____

_____

_____

_____

100 Things I'm Grateful for...

_____

_____

_____

_____

_____

_____

_____

_____

_____

_____

_____

_____

_____

_____

_____

_____

_____

_____

_____

_____

_____

_____

_____

The Power of Faith

100 Things I'm Grateful for...

_____

_____

_____

_____

_____

_____

_____

_____

_____

_____

_____

_____

_____

_____

_____

_____

_____

_____

_____

100 Things I'm Grateful for...

_____

_____

_____

_____

_____

_____

_____

_____

_____

_____

_____

_____

_____

_____

_____

_____

_____

_____

_____

The Power of Faith

Date: _____

_____

_____

_____

_____

_____

_____

_____

_____

_____

_____

_____

_____

_____

_____

5 things I am grateful for:

5 things I love about me:

My intention:

My successes:

What have I manifested or what will I attract into my life today:

What powerful connection will or did I make today?

The Power of Faith

Wake up every morning knowing something magical is about to happen!
Faith Young

Date: _____

_____

_____

_____

_____

_____

_____

_____

_____

_____

_____

_____

_____

_____

_____

_____

5 things I am grateful for:

5 things I love about me:

My intention:

My successes:

What have I manifested or what will I attract into my life today:

What powerful connection will or did I make today?

The Power of Faith

> # "Make sure
> # to make yourself
> # a priority
> # in your life!"
>
> *Faith Young*

Date: _____

_____

_____

_____

_____

_____

_____

_____

_____

_____

_____

_____

_____

_____

_____

5 things I am grateful for:

5 things I love about me:

My intention:

My successes:

What have I manifested or what will I attract into my life today:

What powerful connection will or did I make today?

The Power of Faith

Thank you
for the Reminder
Something Better
Is on its
Way!

FAITH YOUNG

Date: _____

_____
_____
_____
_____
_____
_____
_____
_____
_____
_____
_____
_____
_____
_____
_____
_____

5 things I am grateful for:

5 things I love about me:

My intention:

My successes:

What have I manifested or what will I
attract into my life today:

What powerful connection will or did I make
today?

The Power of Faith

Date: _____

_____

_____

_____

_____

_____

_____

_____

_____

_____

_____

_____

_____

_____

_____

_____

_____

_____

5 things I am grateful for:

5 things I love about me:

My intention:

My Successes:

What have I manifested or what will I
attract into my life today:

What powerful connection will or did I make
today?

The Power of Faith

"Silent gratitude doesn't
do anyone any good"

Faith Young
author of
"What Would Faith Do?"

WWFD.me

Date: _____

_____

_____

_____

_____

_____

_____

_____

_____

_____

_____

_____

_____

_____

_____

_____

Faith Young - The Journal

5 things I am grateful for:

5 things I love about me:

My intention:

My successes:

What have I manifested or what will I
attract into my life today:

What powerful connection will or did I make
today?

The Power of Faith

"Generosity is giving without expectation."

Faith Young
author of What Would Faith Do?

Date: _____

_____

_____

_____

_____

_____

_____

_____

_____

_____

_____

_____

_____

_____

_____

_____

5 things I am grateful for:

5 things I love about me:

My intention:

My successes:

What have I manifested or what will I
attract into my life today:

What powerful connection will or did I make
today?

The Power of Faith

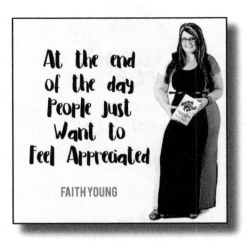

Date: _____

_____
_____
_____
_____
_____
_____
_____
_____
_____
_____
_____
_____
_____
_____
_____
_____
_____

what would Faith Do?

5 things I am grateful for:

5 things I love about me:

my intention:

my successes:

what have I manifested or what will I
attract into my life today:

what powerful connection will or did I make
today?

The Power of Faith

At the end of the day People Just Want to Feel Appreciated

FAITH YOUNG

Date: _____

_____

_____

_____

_____

_____

_____

_____

_____

_____

_____

_____

_____

_____

_____

_____

5 things I am grateful for:

5 things I love about me:

My intention:

My Successes:

What have I manifested or what will I
attract into my life today:

What Powerful connection will or did I make
today?

The Power of Faith

I do not believe in competition!

I believe in ABUNDANCE!

Faith Young
What Would Faith Do?

Date: _____

_____

_____

_____

_____

_____

_____

_____

_____

_____

_____

_____

_____

_____

_____

_____

What would Faith Do?

5 things I am grateful for:

5 things I love about me:

MY intention:

MY Successes:

What have I manifested or what will I attract into my life today:

What Powerful connection will or did I make today?

The Power of Faith

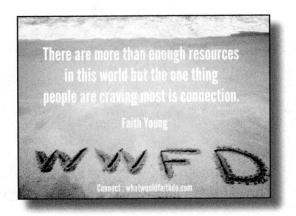

There are more than enough resources in this world but the one thing people are craving most is connection.

Faith Young

W W F D

Connect : whatwouldfaithdo.com

Date: _____

_____

_____

_____

_____

_____

_____

_____

_____

_____

_____

_____

_____

_____

_____

_____

_____

5 things I am grateful for:

5 things I love about me:

My intention:

My successes:

What have I manifested or what will I
attract into my life today:

What powerful connection will or did I make
today?

The Power of Faith

I am open,
willing, and able
to receive.

Faith Young

www.OunceOfFaith.com

Date: _____

_____

_____

_____

_____

_____

_____

_____

_____

_____

_____

_____

_____

_____

_____

_____

5 things I am grateful for:

5 things I love about me:

My intention:

My Successes:

What have I manifested or what will I
attract into my life today:

What powerful connection will or did I make
today?

The Power of Faith

LOVE IS THE SOLUTION!

www.WhatWouldFaithDo.com

Date: _____

_____

_____

_____

_____

_____

_____

_____

_____

_____

_____

_____

_____

_____

_____

_____

Faith Young - The Journal

5 things I am grateful for:

5 things I love about me:

My intention:

My successes:

What have I manifested or what will I
attract into my life today:

What powerful connection will or did I make
today?

The Power of Faith

Date: _____

_____

_____

_____

_____

_____

_____

_____

_____

_____

_____

_____

_____

_____

_____

_____

_____

5 things I am grateful for:

5 things I love about me:

My intention:

My Successes:

What have I manifested or what will I attract into my life today:

What Powerful connection will or did I make today?

The Power of Faith

I AM

_____

(Fill in the Blank)

www.OunceOfFaith.com

Date: _____

_____

_____

_____

_____

_____

_____

_____

_____

_____

_____

_____

_____

_____

_____

_____

Faith Young - The Journal

5 things I am grateful for:

5 things I love about me:

My intention:

My Successes:

What have I manifested or what will I
attract into my life today:

What powerful connection will or did I make
today?

The Power of Faith

the best WAY
tO teAch ANyONe
ANything iS tO
LeAd by
Example

Faith Young

OuncoOfFaith.com

Date: _____

_____
_____
_____
_____
_____
_____
_____
_____
_____
_____
_____
_____
_____
_____
_____
_____
_____

what would Faith Do?

5 things I am grateful for:

5 things I love about me:

MY intention:

MY successes:

What have I manifested or what will I
attract into my life today:

What powerful connection will or did I make
today?

The Power of Faith

Everyone can shine
on a good day. It's
how you show up
on a bad day that
shows your true

COLORS!

Date: _____

_____

_____

_____

_____

_____

_____

_____

_____

_____

_____

_____

_____

_____

_____

_____

Faith Young - The Journal

5 things I am grateful for:

5 things I love about me:

My intention:

My successes:

What have I manifested or what will I attract into my life today:

What powerful connection will or did I make today?

The Power of Faith

Date: _____

_____

_____

_____

_____

_____

_____

_____

_____

_____

_____

_____

_____

_____

_____

_____

5 things I am grateful for:

5 things I love about me:

My intention:

My Successes:

What have I manifested or what will I
attract into my life today:

What powerful connection will or did I make
today?

The Power of Faith

Everyday is a
an Opportunity to
live that Glorious
Abundant Loving
life we were all
meant to live!
- Faith Young

WWFD.me

Date: _____

_____
_____
_____
_____
_____
_____
_____
_____
_____
_____
_____
_____
_____
_____

Faith Young - The Journal

5 things I am grateful for:

5 things I love about me:

My intention:

My successes:

What have I manifested or what will I
attract into my life today:

What powerful connection will or did I make
today?

The Power of Faith

Set your
intentions without
being attached to the outcome.

www.OunceOfFaith.com

Date: _____

_____

_____

_____

_____

_____

_____

_____

_____

_____

_____

_____

_____

_____

Faith Young - The Journal

what would Faith Do?

5 things I am grateful for:

5 things I love about me:

My intention:

My successes:

What have I manifested or what will I
attract into my life today:

What powerful connection will or did I make
today?

The Power of Faith

Make such a powerful
shift in yourself that it causes
a shift in someone else.

Date: _____

_____

_____

_____

_____

_____

_____

_____

_____

_____

_____

_____

_____

_____

_____

Faith Young - The Journal

5 things I am grateful for:

5 things I love about me:

My intention:

My successes:

What have I manifested or what will I
attract into my life today:

What powerful connection will or did I make
today?

The Power of Faith

I ask for help
when I need it.

Faith Young

Date: _____

_____

_____

_____

_____

_____

_____

_____

_____

_____

_____

_____

_____

_____

_____

5 things I am grateful for:

5 things I love about me:

My intention:

My successes:

What have I manifested or what will I
attract into my life today:

What powerful connection will or did I make
today?

The Power of Faith

Date: _____

_____

_____

_____

_____

_____

_____

_____

_____

_____

_____

_____

_____

_____

_____

_____

5 things I am grateful for:

5 things I love about me:

My intention:

My successes:

What have I manifested or what will I attract into my life today:

What powerful connection will or did I make today?

The Power of Faith

The Universe
is reminding me
I deserved to be
happy!

OunceOfFaith.com

Date: _____

_____
_____
_____
_____
_____
_____
_____
_____
_____
_____
_____
_____
_____
_____
_____

what would Faith Do?

5 things I am grateful for:

5 things I love about me:

My intention:

My Successes:

What have I manifested or what will I
attract into my life today:

What powerful connection will or did I make
today?

The Power of Faith

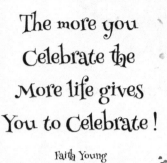

The more you
Celebrate the
More life gives
You to Celebrate !

Faith Young

Date: _____

_____

_____

_____

_____

_____

_____

_____

_____

_____

_____

_____

_____

_____

what would Faith Do?

5 things I am grateful for:

5 things I love about me:

My intention:

My Successes:

What have I manifested or what will I attract into my life today:

What powerful connection will or did I make today?

The Power of Faith

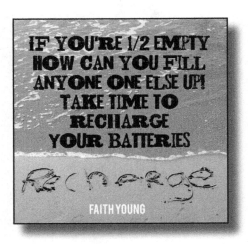

IF YOU'RE 1/2 EMPTY
HOW CAN YOU FILL
ANYONE ONE ELSE UP!
TAKE TIME TO
RECHARGE
YOUR BATTERIES

FAITH YOUNG

Date: _____

_____
_____
_____
_____
_____
_____
_____
_____
_____
_____
_____
_____
_____
_____
_____

Faith Young - The Journal

5 things I am grateful for:

5 things I love about me:

My intention:

My successes:

What have I manifested or what will I attract into my life today:

What powerful connection will or did I make today?

The Power of Faith

Date: _____

_____

_____

_____

_____

_____

_____

_____

_____

_____

_____

_____

_____

_____

_____

_____

5 things I am grateful for:

5 things I love about me:

My intention:

My successes:

What have I manifested or what will I attract into my life today:

What powerful connection will or did I make today?

The Power of Faith

Date: _____

_____
_____
_____
_____
_____
_____
_____
_____
_____
_____
_____
_____
_____
_____
_____
_____

5 things I am grateful for:

5 things I love about me:

my intention:

my successes:

What have I manifested or what will I
attract into my life today:

What powerful connection will or did I make
today?

The Power of Faith

You aRe Ready!
WhaT aRe you
waiting foR?

fAith YOUNg

OUNCEOFFAITH.COM

Date: _____

_____
_____
_____
_____
_____
_____
_____
_____
_____
_____
_____
_____
_____
_____
_____

Faith Young - The Journal

5 things I am grateful for:

5 things I love about me:

My intention:

My Successes:

What have I manifested or what will I
attract into my life today:

What powerful connection will or did I make
today?

The Power of Faith

Date: _____

_____
_____
_____
_____
_____
_____
_____
_____
_____
_____
_____
_____
_____
_____
_____
_____

5 things I am grateful for:

5 things I love about me:

My intention:

My successes:

What have I manifested or what will I
attract into my life today:

What powerful connection will or did I make
today?

The Power of Faith

WHAT IF ALL THIS
uncomfortableness
IS JUST CREATING SPACE
FOR THE REAL
magic
TO START SHOWING UP!

Faith Young

Date: _____

_____
_____
_____
_____
_____
_____
_____
_____
_____
_____
_____
_____
_____
_____
_____
_____
_____

5 things I am grateful for:

5 things I love about me:

My intention:

My Successes:

What have I manifested or what will I attract into my life today:

What Powerful connection will or did I make today?

The Power of Faith

Date: _____

_____

_____

_____

_____

_____

_____

_____

_____

_____

_____

_____

_____

_____

_____

_____

_____

5 things I am grateful for:

5 things I love about me:

My intention:

My Successes:

What have I manifested or what will I
attract into my life today:

What powerful connection will or did I make
today?

The Power of Faith

GO OUT & BE THAT

Badass

YOU WERE MEANT TO BE

www.ounceoffaith.com

Date: _____

_____

_____

_____

_____

_____

_____

_____

_____

_____

_____

_____

_____

_____

_____

_____

5 things I am grateful for:

5 things I love about me:

My intention:

My Successes:

What have I manifested or what will I
attract into my life today:

What powerful connection will or did I make
today?

The Power of Faith

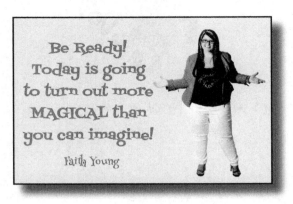

Be Ready!
Today is going
to turn out more
MAGICAL than
you can imagine!

Faith Young

Date: _____

_____
_____
_____
_____
_____
_____
_____
_____
_____
_____
_____
_____
_____
_____
_____

5 things I am grateful for:

5 things I love about me:

My intention:

My successes:

What have I manifested or what will I
attract into my life today:

What powerful connection will or did I make
today?

The Power of Faith

Date: _____

_____

_____

_____

_____

_____

_____

_____

_____

_____

_____

_____

_____

_____

_____

_____

Faith Young - The Journal

5 things I am grateful for:

5 things I love about me:

My intention:

My Successes:

What have I manifested or what will I attract into my life today:

What Powerful connection will or did I make today?

The Power of Faith

luck
HAS NOTHING TO DO WITH IT!

www.ounceoffaith.com

Date: _____

_____

_____

_____

_____

_____

_____

_____

_____

_____

_____

_____

_____

_____

_____

_____

Faith Young - The Journal

5 things I am grateful for:

5 things I love about me:

My intention:

My successes:

What have I manifested or what will I
attract into my life today:

What powerful connection will or did I make
today?

The Power of Faith

Don't
give up!
Good Things
are on
Their way

Faith Young

Date: _____

_____

_____

_____

_____

_____

_____

_____

_____

_____

_____

_____

_____

_____

_____

_____

what would Faith Do?

5 things I am grateful for:

5 things I love about me:

MY intention:

MY Successes:

What have I manifested or what will I attract into my life today:

What Powerful connection will or did I make today?

The Power of Faith

Date: _____

_____

_____

_____

_____

_____

_____

_____

_____

_____

_____

_____

_____

_____

_____

_____

5 things I am grateful for:

5 things I love about me:

My intention:

My Successes:

What have I manifested or what will I
attract into my life today:

What powerful connection will or did I make
today?

The Power of Faith

One of the
most loving things
you can do is love
someone for who
they are.

Faith Young

Date: _____

_____

_____

_____

_____

_____

_____

_____

_____

_____

_____

_____

_____

_____

_____

_____

_____

Faith Young - The Journal

5 things I am grateful for:

5 things I love about me:

My intention:

My successes:

What have I manifested or what will I
attract into my life today:

What powerful connection will or did I make
today?

The Power of Faith

WELCOME
TO MY
magical
LIFE!

whatwouldFaithDo.com

Date: _____

_____

_____

_____

_____

_____

_____

_____

_____

_____

_____

_____

_____

_____

_____

_____

Faith Young - The Journal

5 things I am grateful for:

5 things I love about me:

My intention:

My Successes:

What have I manifested or what will I
attract into my life today:

What powerful connection will or did I make
today?

The Power of Faith

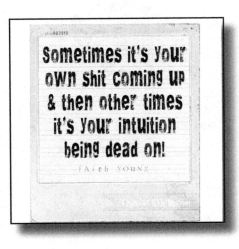

Sometimes it's your own shit coming up & then other times it's your intuition being dead on!

—fAith YOUNG

Date: _____

_____

_____

_____

_____

_____

_____

_____

_____

_____

_____

_____

_____

_____

_____

Faith Young - The Journal

5 things I am grateful for:

5 things I love about me:

My intention:

My Successes:

What have I manifested or what will I
attract into my life today:

What Powerful connection will or did I make
today?

The Power of Faith

If you love
someone enough
you will let them go.
if they love you
enough they will
find their way
back to you!

XOXO

WhatWouldFaithDo.com

Date: _____

_____
_____
_____
_____
_____
_____
_____
_____
_____
_____
_____
_____
_____
_____
_____
_____

5 things I am grateful for:

5 things I love about me:

My intention:

My successes:

What have I manifested or what will I
attract into my life today:

What powerful connection will or did I make
today?

The Power of Faith

The more you appreciate yourself, the more others will appreciate you. Write 100 things you appreciate about yourself

_____

_____

_____

_____

_____

_____

_____

_____

_____

_____

_____

_____

_____

_____

_____

_____

_____

_____

_____

_____

100 Things I Appreciate About Myself...

_____

_____

_____

_____

_____

_____

_____

_____

_____

_____

_____

_____

_____

_____

_____

_____

_____

_____

_____

_____

_____

_____

The Power of Faith

100 Things I Appreciate About Myself...

_____

_____

_____

_____

_____

_____

_____

_____

_____

_____

_____

_____

_____

_____

_____

_____

_____

_____

_____

_____

_____

_____

100 Things I Appreciate About Myself...

_____

_____

_____

_____

_____

_____

_____

_____

_____

_____

_____

_____

_____

_____

_____

_____

_____

_____

_____

_____

_____

_____

_____

The Power of Faith

Note of Appreciation

Thank you for being you! You are as much of a gift to me as I am to you. I'm excited to hear about the gifts that showed up for you in the past 90 days. Your story matters. Once the gifts start showing up, share your story on my *What Would Faith Do? Journal* fan page on Facebook. Better yet, want to inspire others? Take a photo of your journal page and post in on social media daily with your favorite hashtag #WWFD!

Don't stop here! Get your next 90 day #WWFD Journal on Amazon where there are 3 other covers to choose from. Talk about impacting someone's life! What a wonderful way to show you love someone by gifting them one for their next birthday, anniversary, or for a holiday gift!

Loved my 'What Would Faith Do? Journal'? I bet you would fall in love with my book, too. You can get your copy of my "What Would Faith Do?" Book on Amazon on and Kindle.

Could you use a little more Faith on a daily basis? Sign up for my 'Ounce of Faith' to receive free daily inspirational messages right to your email. Go to OunceOfFaith.com say I'm ready & confirm your email and let the magic begin. Follow me on Instagram, Twitter, and on Facebook to receive extra love daily.

Ready to take your life to the next level? Check out my online courses at WhatWouldFaithDo.com. Now you can even download my #WWFD book on audio! Want to meet me in person? Check out my schedule for my next #WWFD workshop online at WhatWould-FaithDo.com.

Feel free to message me at Faith@WhatWouldFaithDo.com

YOU ARE THE KEY TO SPREADING THE LOVE!

Invite your friends to join the What Would Faith Do? Movement.

Let the magic continue....

With a heart full of gratitude much love,

Faith Young

Made in the USA
Middletown, DE
21 April 2022

64609441R00109